IMAGES OF SPORT

RAITH
ROVERS FC
SINCE 1996

IMAGES OF SPORT

RAITH ROVERS FC
SINCE 1996

TONY FIMISTER

TEMPUS

Frontispiece: Four of the first team squad before their first training session of season 1996/97. From left to right: Peter Duffield, Scott Y. Thomson, John Millar and Bobby Geddes.

First published 2004

Tempus Publishing Limited
The Mill, Brimscombe Port,
Stroud, Gloucestershire, GL5 2QG
www.tempus-publishing.com

© Tony Fimister, 2004

The right of Tony Fimister to be identified as the Author
of this work has been asserted in accordance with the
Copyrights, Designs and Patents Act 1988.

British Library Cataloguing in Publication Data.
A catalogue record for this book is available from the British Library.

ISBN 0 7524 3239 7

Typesetting and origination by Tempus Publishing Limited.
Printed in Great Britain.

Contents

Tony Fimister.

Acknowledgements

All of the photographs used in this book were taken by the author, with the exception of the photograph of me at the top of this page (which was taken by the club's video cameraman, Ian Martin).

A book like this, although often looked on as a solo effort, usually involves a number of other people who provide varying amounts of invaluable help. This book is no different and I am glad to be able to take this opportunity to thank them all.

Thank you to: Jim Foy, chairman of the supporters' club, who was able to furnish me with correct name spellings and, often identification of guests, visitors to the club and even obscure players who turned up at Raith Rovers for a very short time, Nigel Ford, who provided research and legal facilities, Fiona Scott and Duncan Peterson of Photo Factory (Kirkcaldy) for their amazingly fast service processing and reprinting some of the photographs in this book, and Terry Adams and Ken Allan at Gallery 42 Kirkcaldy, for the use of the photographic studio.

Also, thank-you to: Brian Jamieson of the Scottish Football League, all the backroom, commercial and administrative staff at Starks Park, the players and management, of which there are too many to name in such a short space, although I would like to give a special thanks to Peter Hetherston and his assistant Kenny Black who were the most helpful and co-operative management team since I joined the club as official photographer, and the chairmen, Alex Penman, Douglas Cromb, Alan Kelly, Danny Smith and Turnbull Hutton, vice chairman/directors Willie Gray, Mario Caira and Eric Drysdale, the programme editors, Gordon Holmes, Allan Dall and Tom Bell, Mike Melville of the official club website, all the sponsors over the last seven seasons who have contributed in some way to the photographs in this book, with a special mention to former club director and main sponsor for many years, Archie Smith of FiFab Glenrothes, long time friend and former assistant commercial manager Sandy McLure, honorary president John Urquhart, who always gives you the time of day to discuss football matters and club video cameramen Ian Martin and Ross Etherington.

Finally I would like to dedicate this book to another team. Whilst I was compiling and writing this book I visited a former Raith Rovers club doctor, Allan Lees, with what I thought was a straightforward minor complaint – thanks to his knowledge and speed I was subsequently seen by consultant Mr A. Ibrahim Amin. His skill, and that of his team at Queen Margaret Hospital Dunfermline, and at the Victoria Hospital Kirkcaldy, meant that I was able to finish this book. I have, during my time at Raith Rovers, witnessed the best and the worst of team work in the greatest sport on earth, but it was during my time under Mr Amin that I really came to know what teamwork is all about.

Introduction

When football is in your blood, you will follow your chosen team through thick and thin. I have always had the greatest of respect for supporters of teams like East Stirling or Albion Rovers – clubs that rarely do well but that have a hard core of followers who keep coming back for more. These supporters know what to expect in a way and if now and again their team manages to put together a good run they know that they are fully entitled to bask in the glory that comes with your team's success.

As a youngster in the 1950s, I lived only a mile from Starks Park and, on match days I could hear the cheers and groans from the large crowds that used to attend matches in those days. I could have chosen to follow any of the bigger clubs, but Raith Rovers were my home team and, at the age of twelve (when my parents allowed me to go to home games), I put on my navy blue and white scarf, bought my first season ticket and never looked back. Through the good and the bad I kept going: never at any time did I say I would not go back, never did I lose the feeling or the hope that good times would follow the bad and, that has been the pattern since those early days of 1962.

When, at the start of season 1991/92 I was asked to take on the role of club photographer, I jumped at the chance. Being able to combine my two hobbies of football and photography was just too good an opportunity to miss and since then I have taken thousands of photographs of the club I love and will always support.

I covered the first five years of my time at the club in the Tempus 'Images of Sport' publication, *Raith Rovers Football Club 1991/92-1995/96*, a period in the club's history that many regard as the their most successful. This publication, following on from those amazing years, covers 1996/97-2002/03. This time the book chronicles the seasons that had Raith Rovers almost going out of business, almost clawing their way back to the Scottish Premier Division, replacing managers and players like they were going out of fashion (the programme editor produced three editions on the trot, each with a different manager in charge) and finally, after just managing to avoid relegation, losing their place in Division One and bouncing back up in just one season as champions of Division Two, under the guidance of the Spaniard, Antonio Calderon.

There have been many times during those seven seasons that I and many like me could have walked away from the club: sadly some did, but I stayed – I kept taking the photographs, kept feeling the highs and lows, happily never losing the feeling that the next match could not come quick enough.

Who knows what the next ten years will bring, how many clubs will survive the financial climate of the new millennium and, if some do fall out of the leagues, who will take their place. All I know is that I will be there taking the photographs or just watching from the stands. This book, I hope, will give Raith Rovers fans, current and lapsed, a chance to re-live those seasons when Raith won the biggest prize of all – they stayed in business.

Tony Fimister
February 2004

Above: Match sponsors 'The neeburs o' Geordie Munro' present the Man of the Match, Raith striker Andy Smith, with an engraved crystal tankard after the home game with Airdrie. Andy scored one of the goals in the 2-1 win. Airdrie were soon to go out of business and reform as Airdrie United after the takeover of Clydebank.

Left: Tuesday 21 January 1997 saw the might of German giants, Bayern Munich, as they took part in a challenge match to open the newly redeveloped Starks Park. Raith won the match 1-0.

one

Three managers, three programmes

Before season 1995/96 had finished, the demolition squads had moved in to take most of Starks Park apart. The first part of the old stadium to come down was the north terracing.

As the weeks passed, the pitch was lifted and levelled and the home end flattened.

Above: Slowly the skeleton of the new north stand rose up to dominate the Pratt Street skyline and the newly-seeded pitch gradually turned from a muddy brown to a lush green rectangle.

Right: Over that sun-filled closed season I took hundreds of photographs of the new-look Starks Park, emerging from the mud and rubble of the shattered old lady that had served the Raith faithfully for over 100 years. Space limits me from including more of these photographs but as pre-season training got under way, the north stand and the new part of the railway stand were ready and the south stand was beginning to take shape. Even the new goal posts were in place and the first lines laid down on the pitch.

I had already taken a team photograph for the season, shot from exactly the same spot as this one, but with a very dull grey background of the north stand without the seats in place. An ever-obliging Jimmy Thomson agreed to let me set up this shot, showing the team in their three sets of strips for the new season.

A couple of young Balwearie High School pupils managed to sneak into the ground during the photocall and persuaded Roary Rover to give them his autograph.

The serious business of pre-season training. Manager Jimmy Thomson and his assistant, Jim McInally, are being helped out by Miodrag Krivokapic and Stevie Kirk.

The league campaign could not have had a tougher start, as Raith were away to the Old Firm for the first two fixtures. A 0-1 defeat at Ibrox was followed by a 1-4 drubbing by Celtic. Sandwiched in between the trips to Glasgow was a 2-3 Coca-Cola Cup loss at the hands of Airdrie. Our first home fixture was against Motherwell and, with the traditional home fans end still under construction, the Raith faithful were allocated the now completed north stand. Motherwell were in no mood to let the home support enjoy the new experience. Two goals from Mitchell Van der Gaag and one from Dougie Arnott saw off the home side 0-3. The defeat was too much for the board and proved to be the last game of which Jimmy Thomson was in charge.

Left: A few days before Aberdeen paid a visit to the new-look Starks Park, Tommy McLean was announced as Jimmy Thomson's replacement.

Below: Tommy McLean's reign as manager lasted just over a week, before he joined his brother Jim at Tannadice – a move that left the Raith Rovers fans and the board somewhat bemused. Before leaving to manage Dundee United, Tommy was able to take charge of the team for the Dons' visit, but could not stop a 1-4 defeat.

Right: The Raith Rovers board of directors moved quickly and Iain Munro was confirmed as Raith's third manager of the season. It was incredible to think that Colin Hume, the programme editor, had produced three programmes in a row, each with a different manager in charge of the club.

Below: A meeting was held in the town's Dean Park Hotel, to introduce Iain Munro to the fans and allow the board to give their reasons behind their decisions for replacing Jimmy Thomson with Tommy McLean, then bringing in Iain. More than two hundred fans attended the meeting and most went home satisfied with the board's answers.

This was my third attempt at taking the team photograph and, hopefully my last one of the season, as everyone at the club was hoping for some stability. Raith had a stadium to be proud of and hopefully a team too.

The ball boys are outnumbered 4-3 by the ball girls as they line up for their group photograph.

The next fixture on the card just had to be a home tie against Dundee United, complete with their new manager Mr T. McLean esq. The atmosphere inside Starks Park was a heady mixture of electricity, expectation and downright hatred as Tommy made his way up the sideline (complete with minder) to take his seat in the away dug out. Whether it was Iain Munro's team talk or just the players reacting to the events of the past few weeks – who knows – but the Kirkcaldy side came out all guns blazing. Even after the home team went behind to a Gary McSwegan goal, you had the feeling that this was still going to be Raith's day, especially when Alex Taylor scored the equaliser from a Tony Rougier pass.

Every Raith player played their part in securing the first points of the season. Alex Taylor scored a second equaliser after David Hannah had given United a half-time 1-2 lead, but Kevin Twaddle netted the winner for Iain Munro's side.

Above: Prior to our home game with the Hearts, club chairman Alex Penman was presented with a cheque for £1.5 million towards the cost of ground redevelopment from the Football Trust and their backers, Littlewoods Pools.

Left: When Raith took to the field for their fourth home fixture of the league campaign against Hearts they sat bottom of the table with only three points from seven starts. Iain Munro had signed three new players, centre half Graham Mitchell (pictured) from Bradford City, midfielder David Lorimer and goalkeeper Colin Scott, both from Hamilton Accies. After going behind to a John Robertson goal in only two minutes, the Rovers rallied and managed a draw when Scott M. Thomson scored his first goal for the club.

The redevelopment of two thirds of the stadium was now complete (except for a lick of paint on the old main stand), so I plucked up the courage to take aerial photographs of the stadium.

I had never flown in a light aircraft before, let alone hang out of the side of the aeroplane as it circled Starks Park. Bill Robertson was my pilot for the flight from Glenrothes airport. Sadly, Bill lost his life along with six others in an air crash at Glasgow a few years after the photographs were taken.

Left: Commercial manager Lynn Penman (left), and office manager Debbie Muir (right), were in the thick of things off the pitch, organising the commercial activities and the day-to-day running of the club.

Below: Although results on the pitch were not going the way the Raith fans wanted, they were at least happier now that they could return to the comparative luxury of the home end, now that the south stand was open for business.

Before the visit of Glasgow Rangers, manager Iain Munro turned to Norwegian football as he tried to safeguard Raith's Premier Division status. Both Vetle Anderson and Kent Bergersen were pitched into the side to face the current champions and both featured well in the 2-2 draw.

One Rangers star who never seemed to perform to the best of his abilities at Starks Park was Paul Gascoigne, but he was always the player that everyone wanted to speak to or be photographed with. In this picture Paul is seen with *Hi-di-Hi*'s Paul McShane having a break after the match in the player's tea room.

Above: Local rivals Dunfermline came, saw and conquered Bert Paton's men, winning 1-2, thanks to a John Millar own goal and Hamish French strike, giving the visitors a 0-2 half-time lead. But when Shaun Dennis was red carded, the home side came more into the game, with Peter Duffield pulling a goal back for Raith, who almost snatched a draw with a few close chances near the end.

Left: It was not just on the pitch that Raith Rovers had new faces – club physiotherapist Gerry Docherty decided to follow Jimmy Nicholl to Millwall and, his position was taken over by one of the most respected backroom men in the Scottish game, John McCreadie.

A good run in the league during November and early December lifted Raith and the supporters, but this was followed by four defeats on the trot. Hearts were our first footers into the new year and, although Danny Lennon opened the scoring (pictured here being swamped by his team-mates) in the first minute, Hearts replied through Robertson and Hamilton to take both points.

Kevin Twaddle helped pull Raith back into the fight for survival with the only goal of the game at Kilmarnock. A two goals to one defeat at home to Celtic was followed by a very entertaining 2-2 draw with Aberdeen at Kirkcaldy. The photograph shows Aberdeen goalkeeper Michael Watt mustering his defence against a Raith attack.

Bayern Munich had promised to officially open the new-look Starks Park and, on Tuesday 21 January 1997, the German giants duly kept their word and the troubles of the league campaign were forgotten for the night.

I have always maintained that if Raith Rovers had been allowed to play their UEFA Cup tie against Bayern Munich at Starks Park instead of Easter Road, things would have been different, as I had always felt that we had lost home advantage. Bayern Munich travelled to Kirkcaldy with a squad worth millions but it was the home side who created the shock, winning 1-0.

The SFA Cup came as a welcome break and Raith recorded a 4-1 victory away to Airdire and a 2-1 Cup win at Brechin, but it was the league results that really counted. Away defeats at the hands of Celtic 0-2, Motherwell 1-5 and Hearts 2-3, kept the team pinned to the bottom of the table. In a do-or-die fixture against the second bottom Kilmarnock on the 1 March, goals from Soren Anderson and Dave Kirkwood helped Raith to a 2-1 win and a precious three points.

Knocked out of the SFA Cup fifth round by First Division Falkirk at Brockville, Raith then lost at home to their rivals, Dunfermline (the fourth time this season that the Pars had taken our scalp). Then they suffered a 1-2 defeat at Tannadice but the Lang Toun lads managed a worthy 1-1 draw at home to Celtic, with David Craig scoring the equaliser in injury time. A week later at Motherwell, the Kirkcaldy side fell to a humiliating 0-5. Raith had started off well but things went disastrously wrong and the result finally condemned Raith to relegation and, for the second time this season, the result against the Steelmen was the last straw for the board and it turned out to be Iain Munro's last game in charge as manager. Worse was to come as the league champions, Rangers, went one better and defeated a sorry Raith side 0-6 in front of their home crowd.

Jimmy Nicholl had returned to Kirkcaldy after a poor season for Millwall had turned bad and, in an effort to boost team spirit, a visit to the Victoria hospital was organised and Jimmy and the players delivered presents to some of the young patients.

The last fixture of a very disappointing season for everyone connected with the Kirkcaldy club was against fellow strugglers Hibs. Before kick-off the Easter Road side were in second bottom place, but equal on points with Motherwell. The game ended in a 1-1 draw. Raith were down, to be replaced by the First Division champions, St Johnstone. Hibs ended the season second bottom of the league, thirteen points clear of Raith. Things looked bleak for the team with chairman Alex Penman looking to sell his shares in the club, but Jimmy Nicholl was back. The question was: could he weave his magic once more and take Raith Rovers back to the Premier division? Only time would tell.

two

Going back never works

Season 1997/98 had not even started when off-the-field activities dominated events at Starks Park. Before the end of the last league campaign, Jimmy Nicholl had been brought back to the Kirkcaldy club by chairman Alex Penman, a move that pleased most of the Raith supporters who hoped that Jimmy would recapture some of his previous successes with the team. Shortly after this move, Alex Penman sold his controlling shares in the club to Alan Kelly, the boss of the club's main sponsor, Kelly's Copiers. Alan Kelly took over as chairman/managing director and brought in Gordon Duncan as a director and he persuaded local solicitor and long standing sponsor of the club, Nigel Ford, to remain as a director. Nigel had been brought on to the board in June of 1997 by Alex Penman after Charles Cant and Bill Sheddon had resigned as directors of the club. The team lined up for the new season's photocall with Alan Kelly and Gordon Duncan seated on the front row, sandwiched between Jimmy Nicholl and Alex Smith.

On Jimmy Nichol's return from Millwall, most of the fans had expected Martin Harvey to return as assistant manager so it came as a bit of a surprise when it was announced that Alex Smith was to be his number one. Jimmy quickly moved into the transfer market, signing goalkeeper Guido Van de Kamp from Dunfermline, Craig McEwan from Clyde and thirty-two year old Keith Wright from Hibs. Keith had previously played for Raith between 1983 and 1986. Part of the deal included midfielder Ian Cameron following Keith Wright from the Edinburgh side and fan's favourite, Tony Rougier, making the opposite journey to the capital.

Unfortunately this is not a photograph left over from the redevelopment of the stadium. A virgin pitch takes about five years to be at its best. The newly-laid pitch, which looked to the untrained eye as coming along nicely, hid an alarming secret. Buried beneath the turf was a drainage system that was of the chocolate fireguard variety. This, coupled with an amazing amount of debris left over from the building site, meant that John Murray, the head groundsman, was left with no alternative but to have the pitch lifted, all the boulders, metal and rubbish removed and a correctly laid drainage system installed.

John's efforts and skill soon produced a pitch fit for the Premier Division and, considering it was grown from seed, it was something of a minor miracle that the playing surface was ready for the start of the season.

Left: The fight for promotion got under way at Stirling on 2 August, but disappointingly Raith could only manage a 1-1 draw. The following Saturday, Forfar came to Starks Park on Coca-Cola Cup duty and, by the end of the day they wished they had not. Peter Duffield turned on an amazing display, scoring a hat-trick in Rovers' 5-0 win. This was Peter's fourth goal in two games, having scored Raith's goal the previous week. His exploits against Forfar earned him the sponsor's Man of the Match award, a football shaped Radio CD player in the sponsor's colours.

Below: Premier Divison Heart of Midlothian,were our third round opponents in the cup and although the visitors ran out winners 1-2, it was Raith's Craig McEwan (seen here with Heart's Steve Foulton) who caught the sponsor's eye, winning the Man of the Match award. More good news was to follow for Craig, the nineteen-year old being named in the Scotland Under-21 squad for the international against Belarus.

When he was manager at Millwall, Jimmy Nicholl had paid Hamilton Accies £380,000 for the services of Paul Hartley. Things did not work out for Paul in London and the unsettled striker left the Den to re-join Jimmy at Kirkcaldy, making his debut against Stranraer in the League Challenge Cup.

By the time St Mirren came to Kirkcaldy, Raith had managed only three draws out of four league starts and were sitting third bottom of the table – the Buddies were in second place. David Craig had returned to Hamilton which allowed the manager to sign former Rover, Jason Dair, from Millwall. Jason went straight into the game against St Mirren, linking up with his brother, Lee. It was a deflected shot from Jason that Lee latched onto, to score one of the home side's goals in the 2-1 win. The sports reporter for the *Fife Free Press* was inspired to write the headline 'Two Dairs Wins'.

Ex-Raith star, Gordon Dalziel, now the Ayr United manager, signed Paul Bonar for a small fee. Paul, who was capped three times for Scotland's Under-21s while he was at Starks Park, was not happy with reserve-team football and the one time Aberdeen target was happy to leave Kirkcaldy if it meant first-team football at Ayr. Jimmy Nicholl quickly replaced Paul with the ex-Rangers player, Kevin Fotheringham, who is seen here with the number 6 on his top, warming up before the match with Falkirk.

The smiles were back on the faces of the fans as Raith slowly climbed the table and, by the time the bottom club, Partick Thistle, came to Kirkcaldy, the home side were up to fourth place.

Raith Rovers have always had the knack of bringing on young players and a new batch of hopefuls put pen to paper in the hope of learning their trade from the likes of Alex Smith and Steve Kirk.

Jason Dair and Craig Dargo look on as Paul Hartley (out of picture) scores for the second game in succession against lowly Stirling Albion.

After four league wins in a row, a 0-1 defeat away to Airdrie had dampened Raith's spirits for the visit of second-placed Dundee, but Raith had risen to third in the table only six points behind the visitors and league leaders Hamilton. But it was not to be and, despite the efforts of Paul Browne in the heart of the defence, the home side went down 0-1.

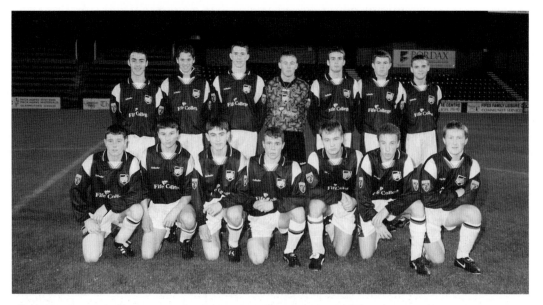

The Youth Team put on an excellent show against Motherwell in the BP Youth Cup, winning by two goals to one. The result was more significant to the Youth Development Officer, Steve Kirk, a former Motherwell player who knew the strength of the youth set up at his former club. The Youth Team development at Starks Park had been greatly helped by a donation of £5,000 from the supporters' club.

Right: This is not a photograph of Jimmy Nicholl giving a rendition of 'Oh Danny Boy' – he is acting as quizmaster at a fund-raising function in the Raith Suite at Starks Park.

Below: Keith Wright followed up his two goals away to Partick with another brace against Hamilton Accies. Even the ex-Rover, David Craig, could do nothing to stop Raith winning 3-1 for the second week in a row. The win kept second-placed Raith in touch with the leaders, Dundee, who had led the league since day one of the campaign.

There is no hiding that feeling of delight as the youngster, Craig Dargo, celebrates the first strike of his hat-trick against St Mirren. Another product of the youth set-up at Kirkcaldy, Craig was about to be released by the club until Jimmy Nicholl returned and talked the board into re-signing him.

The subs warm up during the St Mirren game, hoping for a chance to get in on the action. Jay Stein leads the trot up the sidelines, followed by Jason Dair and the new signing, Andy Galloway. All three were given their chance late on in the game, which Raith won 4-1.

Right: Partick Thistle travelled to Kirkcaldy. They were struggling to avoid relegation and Rovers were five points off the top spot. Before the match I photographed the Partick manager, John McVeigh, deep in conversation with his Raith counterpart. Maybe he was asking Jimmy what it was like to be manager at Starks Park?

Below: When Falkirk visited Raith eleven days earlier on league business, they were in second place and four points clear of the home side. Goals from Danny Lennon and Craig Dargo had helped to close the gap between the clubs. That was followed up with the 2-0 win against Partick Thistle to leapfrog the Rovers into second place. Falkirk came looking for revenge and despite the efforts of Paul Hartley and his team-mates, Raith could not find the form that knocked Hibs out of the cup in the previous round, Alex Totten's men recording a convincing 1-3 win. Raith could now concentrate on their push for promotion.

Our mascots for the Falkirk cup tie were Kirkcaldy sisters, Gemma and Nicola Smith, who are with Danny Lennon.

A new signing, Marvin Andrews, a Trinidad and Tobago international, brought a bit of sunshine into the life of the lottery winner, Christian McIntosh, when along with Jimmy Nicholl he presented Christian with a cheque for £500.

Kevin Fotheringham had been moved back into the centre of the defence, but his striker's instinct was still obvious when he opened the scoring against Airdrie.

Marvin Andrews quickly endeared himself to the Raith fans and although he was often described as Bambi on ice, his strong, honest play added an extra dimension to the team's defence.

Left: Well travelled Andy Walker had joined Raith and was an immediate success, scoring in the 1-0 win away to Falkirk, and again three days later in the 4-1 demolition of Hamilton.

Below: Andy could not keep up his 'goal-a-game' record and for the visit of Gordon Dalziel's Ayr United, it was defences on top. Even the Raith defender, Paul Browne, made his way into the Ayr box in an effort to break the deadlock, but the game ended 0-0.

Above: There were more changes in the backroom staff at Starks Park. John Brownlie and ex-England international, Terry Butcher, joined the coaching staff. The office manager, Debbie Muir, had left to be replaced by the office administrator, Keri Gooding. Although it was too late to make a difference to the league campaign, it was hoped that John and Terry would make a big difference next season.

Right: Nineteen-year-old Jay Stein had started to break into the first team and the 5ft 7in-left-sided-wingman was already showing the skills he had on offer. Jay's first team debut was against Rangers at the end of season 1996/97, in a game that saw Raith lose 0-6 to the champions. Coming on as a sub against Morton, the youngster from Dunfermline impressed the home support, but it was Morton who went home with the three points, winning 1-2.

Above: A local boy, Steve Tosh, recently signed from St Johnstone, also played his first game for Raith against Morton. Steve turned senior when the Arbroath boss, Jocky Scott, signed him from Glenrothes Juniors and a year later went full-time when Paul Sturrock took him to the Perth club. Steve was an uncompromising player and was known for giving one hundred per cent at all times.

Above: Raith regained some pride the following Saturday when they defeated St Mirren 2-0 in Paisley. No one in the home crowd could have expected bottom-of-the-table-Stirling Albion to leave Starks Park with all three points but it seemed Kevin Drinkell's men had a bigger appetite for the game, winning 0-1 and giving the Forth Bank team a slim chance of avoiding relegation.

Right: Commercial manager Allan Paul announced to the Raith faithful a change to the club badge, which caused quite a bit of controversy. The crest of the full lion holding a shield was to revert back to the old Novar crest of the half lion holding a heraldic buckle (shown here). Personally, I was delighted with the news of the change but some Raith fans sporting tattoos of the current badge were a 'wee bit' annoyed.

Opposite below: When Dundee came to Starks Park on 11 April, the Dens park club only needed a draw to win the First Division championship, and second placed Raith were in no mood to let them secure promotion to the Premier Division on their own ground. Back on his old patch was the central defender, Robbie Raeside, who did an excellent job marking Raith's Paul Hartley out of the game at least for most of the time, for it was Paul who grabbed the home side's goal in the 1-1 draw that was enough to send Dundee up to the top division. Although the sight of the thousands of Dundee supporters that had travelled to Kirkcaldy celebrating promotion left you with that sinking feeling, it was nice to see Robbie winning a championship medal and I was one of the first to congratulate him when he came off the pitch.

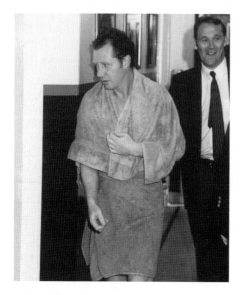

Above left: Our last game of the season was against Hamilton Accies and Jimmy Nicholl was hoping to end the season on a high note. Raith had missed out on promotion to return back to the Premier Division in one season. Falkirk had pipped them for second spot and the compensation that went with it, so all that was at stake was pride. Raith duly restored that pride with a 2-1 win. After the game I caught Jimmy on camera nipping into the press room to give his after-match analysis. Much to the amusement of all in the press room and the hallway, Jimmy appeared dressed only in a couple of towels. The Accies manager, Sandy Clark, saw the funny side of it and so did the rest of us in the hallway as the bottom towel had a large hole in the back.

Above right: Jimmy Nicholl's last act of season 1997/98 was to sign the goalkeeper, Guido Van de Kamp, to a long-term contract. When Jimmy arrived back in Kirkcaldy there were only two players left from the first term of his managerment, Danny Lennon and Davie Kirkwood being the survivors, so it was going to take time for him to build 'his' team. Some pundits had said to Jimmy, 'Going back never works', but that was not his view. Time would tell, and with his new backroom staff in place and some new players on the horizon, I for one could not wait for next season to start.

Left: What a backroom staff for any team to have! From left to right, back row: John Valente (kit man), Alex Smith (assistant manager), Terry Butcher (coach). Front row: John Brownlie (youth coach), Jimmy Nicholl (manager) and John McCreadie (physio). With a team like that how could you fail?

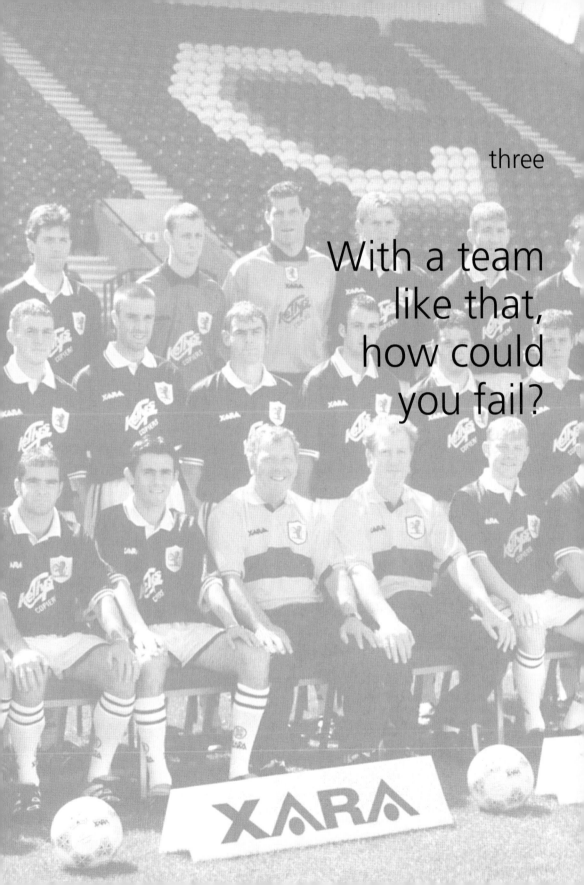

three

With a team
like that,
how could
you fail?

The first team pool for season 1998/99. From left to right, back row: G. McCulloch, K. Byers, I. Cameron, D. Wilson, G. Van de Kamp, P. Browne, K. Wright, J. Dair. Middle row: J. Brownlie, D. Bowman, R. Yaylor, G. Mitchell, L. Dair, A. Hynd, C. Smart, J. Stein, R. Venables, J. McCreadie. Front row: T. Butcher, D. McPherson, C. McEwan, P. Hartley, A. Smith, J. Nicholl, S. Tosh, K. Fotheringham, D. Lennon, J. Valente.

The Youth players under the management of John Brownlie and Terry Butcher are lined up for their photocall. The first team and the Youth photocall are usually a bit of a shambles but this season it went as smoothly as any photographer could hope for. Then again, what player would dare fool around, with the likes of Terry Butcher and Alex Smith in control?

Above: The groundsman, John Murray, tends to his grass-cutting machine, as steel erecters put the finishing touches to a protective frame around the police control box. The steel frame was not to protect the police from hostile fans – it was to stop rusting metal falling from the main stand roof onto their control room. Although the stadium had been redeveloped the main stand had hardly been touched and was now deemed unsafe for use – at least until maintenance was carried out.

Right: The new signing, Dave Bowman, did some ball juggling while I took his photograph for the programme. The programme editor thought that this photograph showed Dave at his best, but I was not so cruel and supplied him with a conventional photograph. I mean, if this photograph had managed to go to print, you can just imagine the shouts from his team-mates 'Hey! Ba' heid gies' a pass' – or something like that. Dave had been with Dundee United for twelve years and it was expected his experience would help Raith win promotion. It was also hoped that Ally McCoist would join the club, but that failed to materialise.

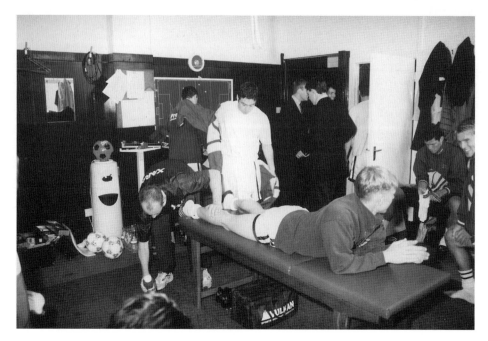

When it comes to football I am very superstitious and I do not like to go anywhere near the dressing room on a match day. Every time I do, the team suffers a defeat but I thought if I went in to photograph the pre-match ritual, it would not matter as it was only a friendly against Fulham. Wrong! Fulham gave the home side a lesson in attacking football, beating Raith 1-4.

The team captains line up with the mascots and local referee, John Rowbotham, before the kick-off against Fulham. (John is the one with the whistle around his neck).

After two home defeats to Fulham and Hamilton, the home support hoped for a change in fortunes when Hearts came to Kirkcaldy for a friendly. Greig McCulloch ran non-stop, helping the defence to keep the Hearts forwards at bay.

Ian Cameron managed to get on the score sheet as Raith cruised past a strong Hearts side, winning 4-2. In this photograph, Ian and Jason Dair shadow Hearts trialist Simone Baldo.

Davie Kirkwood, Danny Lennon and Craig Dargo, all sidelined through injury, look on as their team-mates lose 0-2 to Hamilton in the opening league fixture.

Clydebank's Fraser Wishart slides in on Paul Hartley in the League Cup second round tie, which the home side went on to win. Raith lost Craig McEwan to a red card, but Clydebank had to play for seventy-three minutes without ex-Raith goalkeeper Colin Scott, who was knocked unconscious and had to be replaced by outfield player Craig Taggart, as Clydebank did not have a substitute goalie.

Raith Rovers had entered a team in the Reserve League East and kicked off their fixtures with a superb 4-0 win at home to Forfar. Outstanding in a youthful Raith side was Craig Smart, who scored two of the goals, one from the penalty spot after he had been brought down in the box by Forfar's Rattray.

Paul Shields made his debut for Raith against Ayr United. He could not help Raith win, but at least the 0-0 draw won the Rovers' first point of the season. Paul is seen here keeping two Ayr defenders busy, as Keith Wright signals to a team-mate where he wants the ball.

Raith Rovers made a little bit of history when they became the first away team to win at Airdrie's new home, the Shyberry Excelsior Stadium. They won 1-0 thanks to a Paul Hartley goal with only ten minutes to go. Then it was back to Kirkcaldy to take on the bottom club, Morton. Despite Jimmy Nicholl's coaching from the sideline, the points were shared in a disappointing 0-0 draw. It was the third home league game in a row in which Raith had failed to score.

Raith Rovers' financial problems were becoming more acute by the day and the supporters' club came to the rescue once again, donating a cheque for £20,000. The photograph shows the directors, Willie Gray (left) and Nigel Ford (right), receiving the cheque from Brian Fairfull, the chairman of the supporters' club. Willie Gray, who had resigned as a director at the end of the last season, had returned to the board when Alan Kelly took control of the club. Another fundraising venture that was offered by the club was the chance to purchase a lifetime season ticket for £1,175. Almost one hundred fans (including myself) took the chance to help out the club. It was also announced that Terry Butcher had left the club and was to join the backroom staff at Dundee United. This was seen by fans as a cost-cutting exercise. Due to the results, and being second bottom of the division, crowds were down. A huge rise in the price of sponsorship imposed on the commercial department had made it harder for Allan Paul and his team to attract new and traditional sponsors to the club. Financially, and football wise, Raith were on a very dangerous downward spiral.

The Bankies were back but this time it was on league business. Paul Hartley made a nuisance of himself in the Clydebank box at this corner, but again Raith failed to score at home and the visitors snatched all three points, winning by the only goal of the game.

For the visit of the St Mirren manager, Jimmy Nicholl turned to the young guns to help turn around Raith's season, introducing Craig Smart, Kevin Byers, Jay Stein and George Fotheringham to the first team. Although it was the veteran Keith Wright who scored the only goal of the game, it was the youngsters who really impressed, with Craig Smart acting as a constant thorn in the Buddies' defence.

Gerry Britton made the short journey from the west of Fife when he came to Starks Park on loan from Dunfermline. Gerry did not manage to get on the score sheet but he was instrumental in helping Raith win the three points on offer. Paul Hartley converted a first half penalty and Craig Dargo wrapped up the points with a last minute goal to finish the game at 2-0. Gerry won the Man of the Match award for his efforts.

By mid-December, Alan Kelly's reign as chairman/managing director came to an end and the director, Willie Gray, moved quickly to bring in the experienced Douglas Cromb to take charge of the club. Raith were in free fall both on and off the park. The arrival of Douglas Cromb and Iain Brennan as commercial director was to be the turning point in the club's fortunes. A 'save the Rovers' campaign had already been launched and the new board, made up of mainly true Raith Rovers supporters, was determined to do just that – save the Rovers. This photograph shows the new board taking their places in the directors' box. From left to right, front row: John Brownlie (youth coach), Alex Smith (assistant manager), Douglas Cromb (chairman/managing director), Iain Brennan (commercial director), Willie Gray (vice chairman), Jim Whyte (director). Middle row: Mario Caira (director), Fraser Hamilton (director) and Eric Drysdale (secretary).

Out of the darkness came a glimmer of light – four glimmers, in fact, as Raith Rovers proudly paraded their young Scottish international players at a photocall. From left to right: Kevin Nicholl – Under-16s, Craig Dargo and Craig McEwan – Under-21s, and Paul Shields – Under-18s.

The players did their best to help raise the club's profile in the community when they appeared at the sportswear store, JJB Sports, in the town's retail park. Craig Dargo autographs a young fan's 1999 calendar as Greig McCulloch, Danny Lennon and Kevin Byers look on.

Above: Ian Cameron's header beats Morton goalkeeper Ally Maxwell, as Raith equalise to make the score 1-1. Unfortunately the new board was not to see any rewards for the home side's efforts. Inspired by the ex-Raith forward, Kevin Twaddle, Morton went on to win 1-3.

Left: Jimmy Nicholl and two young fans model some of the new Raith merchandise on sale in the club shop. The 'new' club crest can be seen on training tops but the supporters' club scarves still used the badge with the full lion with the shield.

Above: It is not very often that Marvin Andrews looks small – he must be one of the tallest players on the books at Starks Park, but he was dwarfed by Falkirk's 6ft 7in central defender, Kevin James. Falkirk came to Kirkcaldy sitting second top of the league, eight points adrift of leaders Hibs. Raith were second from bottom, but a tremendous fight back gave Rovers the three points. After going behind to an early Scott Crabbe deflected goal, Ian Cameron headed Raith's equaliser, and, deep into injury time, the Hearts on-loan striker, Derek Holmes, rifled home the winner.

Right: The match sponsors for the Falkirk game, First Scottish Searching Services of Edinburgh, chose the Raith defender, Marvin Andrews, as their Man of the Match. Joining Marvin and a representative of First Scottish is the ex-Raith and Dunfermline manager, Bert Paton (right).

I cannot imagine the total number of people who have served Raith Rovers since I joined them as club photographer at the start of season 1991/92. The vast number of players, managers, directors, backroom staff, admin and commercial staff, would frighten any human resources manager, but occasionally some people do manage to stay for at least a few years. Tony Coventry has assisted a few groundsmen in his time with the club. The kit man, John Valente, as well as producing award-winning fish suppers in his full-time occupation as one of Scotland's best known fish friers, has laid out the kit for numerous players, but the man with the golden voice (well, gold plated), the match announcer Drew Nairn, was in with the bricks, or so we thought. All good things must come to an end, however, and Drew chose the Scottish Cup third round tie against Clyde to announce to the fans that this was to be his last game. Gordon Adamson (pictured) had the unenviable task of trying to reach Drew's high standards.

Right: Derek Holmes was cup tied for the visit of Clyde. Whether his inclusion would have made any difference is hard to say, as a fired up Clyde dominated the game, winning 0-4. Derek was back in the starting line-up for the next game, when Raith played host to Clydebank. The Hearts striker put in a hard shift and helped Rovers to a convincing 2-1 win.

Right: Before our match with Airdrie, Christie Smith of match sponsors Fife Fabrication got 'up close and personal' with mascot Roary Rover (Roary had to sit down with a brandy-laced cup of tea after that photograph).

Below: Unfortunately the game against Airdrie went against us with the Coca-Cola Cup hero, Scott Thomson, now plying his trade with the Diamonds, shutting out the Raith forwards. Gareth Evans latched onto a short pass back from Kevin Fotheringham, to score the only goal of the game.

Above: The Rovers revival fund was growing by the week with every kind of conceivable activity being tried to boost the fund. Some were large and some were small but all contributions helped to keep the club afloat. Auchmuty High School pupils, Alex Latto, Richard McGregor and Ben Reekie, organised a sponsored football match with friends and collected £295.20 to add to the fund. I photographed the lads handing over the cheque to the chairman, Douglas Cromb, and assistant manager, Alex Smith.

Below: Friendly matches against Hearts, Aberdeen and Rangers were played at Starks Park to raise funds, with mixed fortunes for the home side. Hearts fielded a full strength team winning 0-3. The Aberdeen side was described by the programme editor as experienced, but fell to a determined Raith Rovers, with the home side reversing the Hearts score with goals from Dargo, Stein and Holmes. Even when Aberdeen did manage a rare attack on goal, they found a gloved Marvin Andrews hard to get past.

Above: Rangers fielded a strong team for their fundraising friendly and, more importantly attracted a crowd of almost 5,000 to help the revival fund. The Rangers stars did not really break sweat in the early part of the game but, when in the sixty-ninth minute a spectacular flick from Steve Tosh beat Stefan Klos in the Rangers goal, the champions-elect stepped up a gear. The goal seemed to give the home side a big confidence boost and, much to the annoyance of the manager Dick Advocaat, his multi-million-pound forwards could not find a way past the Rovers rearguard, with nineteen-year-old Laurie Ellis outstanding on the left side of the Raith defence. In fact, Laurie marked Andrei Kanchelskis out of the game, and the friendly ended 1-0. The smiles on the home fans' faces as they left the ground were broadened as the announcer Gordon Adamson relayed the score from the Hamilton *v.* Ayr Utd game in which Ayr won 2-0. This result kept the home side four points clear of second bottom Hamilton.

Below: Bottom club Stranraer were finally relegated by Raith, but they fought all the way and it was a scrambled goal in injury time from Craig Dargo that put paid to their challenge, and Raith won 3-2. The pick of the goals was Kevin Fotheringham's nineteenth minute headed goal from Steve Tosh's corner.

Above: More fundraising. This time a casino night was held in the Raith Suite. The commercial executive, Jennifer Tottenham, is seen here handing over a bottle of champagne to one lucky winner.

Left: Players and supporters' club members lent a hand, and Guido Van de Kamp even acted as barman. Seconds after I took this photograph he dropped the glass he was drying and Jimmy Nicholl substituted him.

The supporters' club organised a challenge match in aid of the fund, and a very impressive Jimmy Nicholl XI lined up for this photograph. From left to right, back row: Jimmy Nicholl, Colin Harris, Paul Smith, Jock McStay, Cammy Fraser, George McGeachie and John Valente. Front row: Gordon Dalziel, Andy Harrow, Craig Coyle, Dave Narey and Peter Hetherston.

Their opponents for the challenge match were Raith Rovers Amateur Football Club, captained by Gavin Quinn. The amateur side gave a good account of themselves but the 'Old Boys' (apologies to Craig Coyle) ran out comfortable winners 7-2.

Above: Raith did find some success on the field during this very difficult season. A very young side had easily won the East of Scotland Reserve League and they did manage another piece of silverware when they won the Fife Cup, beating Burntisland Shipyard 5-0 in the final. Kevin Byers accepted the trophy on behalf of the club.

Left: The Chancellor of the Exchequer, Gordon Brown, had, as a fourteen-year old, sold programmes at Starks Park. On his visit to Kirkcaldy he took the opportunity to relive his past employment, at least for the sake of the massed ranks of press photographers that turned up. To put Raith's financial troubles into perspective, the 'save the Rovers' fund was suspended for the game, to allow volunteers to collect for the Kosovo appeal.

After the photocall, Gordon Brown paid a visit to the supporters' club shop to purchase a team strip. I am not sure if he actually offered to buy the former East Fife player, Henry McLeish, a Rovers top but by the look on the faces of the supporters' club officials, the answer was no!

League Champions, Hibs, were the visitors for the match Gordon Brown had picked to watch, and he must have returned home disappointed, as the only high point in this match was Derek Holmes' goal. Steve Tosh's shot was only parried by the Hibs' goalkeeper and Derek was on hand to blast home. After that, Hibs cruised to run out winners 1-3.

The final home game of the season brought St Mirren to Kirkcaldy. Raith were six points clear of second bottom Hamilton and they had the luxury of a better goal difference with only two games to go. The game ended in a 1-1 draw and that point meant First Division football for another season at least. The *Fife Free Press* reporter, Gordon Holmes, had the dubious pleasure of touring Scotland to cover all of Raith's matches for his newspaper. Always entertaining and informative, Gordon also contributed to the club's matchday programme. Even an experienced reporter like Gordon had a problem trying to whip up enthusiasm for a team that looked to be going nowhere but down. Raith had just managed to avoid relegation and there was still a financial mountain to climb to save the club, but Raith were still in business and still in the First Division. I, like all true Raith fans, did not want to suffer the strain and embarrassment of another relegation fight. In his article, 'View from the press box' in the programme, Gordon urged the management team to build for the future. Our youngsters had performed in their League better than the seniors – maybe the future was at the club already. Many questions were asked about the failures of this season, but most went unanswered. The main question though, was how could the management team have failed so miserably? The CVs of the likes of Jimmy Nicholl, Alex Smith, John Brownlie and for a short while Terry Butcher, were remarkable, but they just could not make it work at Starks Park. Was it a case of too many cooks, or was it the failure of those directing the club that had caused Raith's fall from grace? All the faithful fans really knew was that their team was only a shadow of the Raith Rovers that had, in the not-so-distant past, entertained the likes of Bayern Munich, won a major trophy and regularly filled the stadium. The times they were 'a-changing' and this was only the start for British teams. Players' wage bills were outstripping many clubs' income and soon Partick Thistle, Falkirk, Airdrie, Clydebank, Motherwell, Dundee, Livingston, near neighbours Dunfermline and a clutch of clubs in England and the rest of Europe, would be struggling for survival. No one wants to see any club go to the wall but, at this point, the supporters of Raith Rovers Football Club were only concerned with the problems of the team from the Langtoun.

four

At least the 'Pars' couldn't beat us!

During the summer of 1999, I was invited to a press conference. Vice chairman, Willie Gray, introduced me to the new manager, John McVeigh, and his assistant Peter Hetherston, and more importantly to the new owner and managing director of the club, the west coast businessman, Danny Smith. As the new management team and the new board took their places in front of the cameras and reporters, I realised that this was to be the start of a new era for the club, but the question was, was it to be a good or a bad era? The picture shows the line-up that faced the media. From left to right: Mario Caira (director), Peter Hetherston (assistant manager), Danny Smith (managing director), Willie Gray (chairman), John McVeigh (manager) and Eric Drysdale (company secretary). Some of the media turned up at Starks Park for the announcement of the new owners and management team. To see so many journalists, reporters and photographers in Kirkcaldy at one time meant only one thing – it was a very quiet news day. Normally the first cut of the Ibrox pitch or a Celtic player cutting his toenails attracts more interest than a 116-year-old football club being saved from extinction. Still, Raith enjoyed the attention while it lasted.

John McVeigh and Peter Hetherston set about reorganising the playing staff and bringing in new faces. Paul Tosh, Kevin Gaughan, Steve Hamilton, Paul Agnew and Alex Burns were all given contracts, and the experienced veteran, Kenny Black, left troubled Airdrie to join Raith as a player/youth coach.

Another new 'manager' to appear at Starks Park was the Hollywood legend, Robert Duval. 'Bob' had enlisted the help of John McVeigh and some of the Raith players in the making of his film, *The Cup*, which was all about a wee Scottish club called Kilnockie FC, who managed to reach the Scottish Cup final against the Glasgow giants, Rangers. Everyone at Starks Park was thrilled to see the film star going about his business, researching how a typical Scottish manager plied his trade. Understandably, I was in demand for the obligatory photocall. 'Bob' lines up with the board members. From left to right: Danny Smith, Mario Caira, Robert Duvall, Willie Gray, Colin McGowan and Eric Drysdale. The film was eventually released as *A Shot at Glory*. The only person that I know who actually managed to see it was Kenny Black, and he rated it as 'okay'!

Being a true professional, the Oscar winning Mr Duvall did not miss an opportunity to publicise the film and took this chance to do a piece to camera. The film, produced and directed by Michael Corrente, also stared Ally McCoist and Rovers players Davie Kirkwood, Steve Hamilton, Kevin Gaughan, Kenny Black, Craig McEwan and the assistant manager, Peter Hetherston. Also included in the latter stages of the film, playing for Rangers, was Raith's new signing, Didier Agathe.

The new signing, Paul Tosh, in pre-season action

Early season results were mixed – a slim 1-0 win in the CIS Cup away to Stranraer, a 1-1 draw at Livingston, followed by a 1-0 home win in the Bell's Challenge cup against Ayr United. Then St Mirren decided to take a belated revenge on Raith for that 7-0 drubbing, back at the start of season 1992/93. The Paisley Buddies ran out winners by six goals to nil. After the game, some of the jubilant St Mirren players admitted that they were stunned by the way the home fans applauded them off the pitch at the end of the game. Obviously disappointed by the result, the Rovers fans at least were sporting enough to acknowledge a good team producing a magnificent result.

That drubbing at the hands of St Mirren was put aside when, four days later, Premier Division Motherwell were Raith's opponents in the second round of the CIS League Cup. The score was 2-2 at ninety minutes, but Raith finally succumbed 4-5 in the penalty shoot-out. Andy Clark was given a surprise start for the first time that season. They were out of the cup, but the home side had at least regained some pride, and showed that they had the look of a team that could achieve something.

There were more changes, this time in the office. Keri Gooding had left the club to be replaced by Billy McPhee, returning for a second spell. Pat McAuley was running the commercial team, but it was the on-the-field activity that interested the fans. Raith had a new star in Didier Agathe, from the French club, Montpellier. I watched Didier in a closed door bounce match when he arrived in Kirkcaldy and he impressed the management so much that he was included in the team for the next game against Airdrie. If he was looking for a good start he certainly managed that, scoring a hat-trick on his debut. The following week, in front of his home crowd, he scored again as Raith took Ayr United 'to the cleaners', winning 5-1.

Above: With six games played in the League, Raith were lying in sixth place. Their record at this point was: won two, drawn two, lost two, but all that was forgotten when Dunfermline came to visit. Some people would say of Scotland that they can lose to any team as long as they beat England – it is the same with Raith and the 'Pars'. I have said it before, I am superstitious, bad things happen if I go into the dressing room before a game, but when John McVeigh tells you to go into the dressing room and take a photograph of the mascot with the team you do not argue, and eleven-year-old Ian Duff was duly photographed with the players. I can tell you it is hard enough taking photographs, without trying to do it with everything crossed, and where do you get lucky white heather at short notice?

Below: 'To the game', where Dunfermline had the ex-Raith star, Jason Dair, in their ranks. During the last season, Jason had become one of the cost-cutting casualties of the club's dire financial position. Subsequently he was signed by the 'Pars' and had managed eight games in the Premier Division before the West Fife club were relegated. Two goals from Craig Dargo had given Raith a comfortable and deserved lead and I thought that all my finger-crossing in the dressing room had paid off. Unfortunately the jinx was still working and the visitors managed to score two goals to take a share of the points. After the game, John McVeigh banned me from the dressing room on match days.

Above: The most memorable part of the game at home to Falkirk was not Craig Dargo's two goals – which secured the three points for Raith in the 2-1 win – but the antics of Falkirk's club doctor, who ran onto the pitch in the most dramatic manner ever witnessed in my time at Starks Park, not once but twice. The injured Falkirk player required attention but that job is usually left to the physio on the pitch, who, if necessary, will call on the assistance of the doctor if it looks bad. Whether the Bairns doc' was auditioning for *Casualty*, or had been taking lessons in histrionics from Alex Totten I do not know, but his performance certainly added an edge to this game. The Falkirk doctor is on the far left of the photograph (the man in the suit with the wide parting in his hair). Just above him on the closed terracing were the massed ranks of the press reporters. With the main stand out of action because of work on the roof, the scribes went back to their roots and pretended to be just like real supporters, all except Gordon Holmes who wrote for the *Fife Free Press* and the club programme. Gordon took up residency in the pie stand (far right of the picture) for the duration of the repairs.

Below: The team photocall had been postponed because of torrential rain, so we were well into the season when the team lined up behind the new sponsor's board.

Newly promoted Livingston were performing well in the First Division, sitting third in the table when they paid Raith a visit. The home side were in no mood to let the newcomers show their skills and Raith won the match 3-1. The two Pauls – Browne and Shields – scored a goal each, and Kenny Black thumped a penalty past the stand-in goalkeeper, Brian Mcphee, after the Livingston custodian saw red. In the background the new roof starts to cover the skeleton of the main stand covering.

Alex Burns had made the number ten shirt his own with a string of classy performances and was fast becoming a favourite of the home fans.

The ex-Raith player, Keith Wright, now with Morton, seems to have had a ticklish nose as he tried to get in between a very determined looking Steve Tosh and Craig McEwan. Raith registered a second successive 3-1 win in this game. Agathe, Burns and Stein scored for Rovers.

Jay Stein was on the score sheet again when Raith travelled to Dunfermline for the Fife derby. Unfortunately his goal only earned the team one point in a 1-1 draw, but Rovers got back to winning ways eight days later when they travelled to Ayr for an unusual Sunday game. Brian Hetherston scored the only goal of the match. The following Saturday, as I celebrated my fiftieth birthday, the team let me down – no birthday card, no cake and only one point in a 1-1 draw with Airdrie. At least Marvin Andrews was on form, in fact he was head and shoulders above his opponents.

Above: Brian 'Bubbles' Hetherston had come off the bench to score the winner the week before at Ayr and he repeated the act against Airdrie after he came on for Paul Tosh. Bubbles is seen here with representatives of the *Daily Record*, who were the match ball sponsors.

Left: The result against Inverness kept Raith in touch with the league leaders, St Mirren, and second place Dunfermline, but this result and our league placing was soon forgotten when the news broke that the manager John McVeigh had left the club. Accusations were met by counter-accusations, as both sides of the argument were plastered across the tabloids. John McVeigh claimed he was sacked, the club claimed he resigned. A 0-1 defeat away to Morton compounded Raith's off-the-field problems. Peter Hetherston had been given the manager's job and the ex-Raith boss, Frank Connor, was brought in to guide him through the transitional period.

If anything can bring the smile back onto the face of any football supporter it is a derby day win, especially if it is the new year derby, and that is exactly what Raith did. Dunfermline had performed steadily all season, tucking in behind the league leaders St Mirren, who, by the turn of the year had only lost two games. But it was the home side who turned on the style and the sizeable travelling support from the west of Fife could only look on in dismay, as Raith bulged the visitors' net three times.

Even the Pars top scorer, Owen Coyle, and his team-mate, the ex-Rover Steve Crawford, could not find a way past the home defence, in which Marvin Andrews was outstanding.

Didier Agathe, seen here in Raith's next game against Ayr United, had been outstanding in the derby game and was attracting the attention of a number of Premier Division clubs.

Whipping up enthusiasm on a freezing winter's day is sometimes a difficult task, so the club brought in Andy Gillies and his trumpet to stir up the fans.

Above: At the start of the season the physiotherapist John McCreadie had left to join Dundee and his place was taken by John Cooper. John opened up the physio room to the general public every Thursday evening to help anyone with a sport-related injury. I took this photograph for a local newspaper, to publicise the opening of the sports injury clinic, and a couple of ice hockey players from Fife Flyers came along to check out the facilities. Marvin Andrews, who is lying on the physio's couch, was not in need of treatment – he was just tired! The line-up in the treatment room is, horizontal: Marvin Andrews, and standing from left to right: John Cooper, Todd Duitame and Russell Monteith.

Right: John also formed links with the Club One Fitness health club in the town, who had offered the use of their facilities and fitness equipment to Raith Rovers.

The roof on the main stand was finally finished and new lighting and seats had been installed to bring the stadium up to Premier Division requirements. The ugly frame and cover over the police control box had also been removed, as there was now no chance of anything other than pigeon droppings falling from above.

The striker, Paul Tosh, had returned from a loan spell with Arbroath and was included in the starting line-up for the game against St Mirren. There was to be no repeat of the 0-6 scoreline that had haunted Raith Rovers players and fans alike since the first home league game of the season. Both team's defences were on top in a hard, sometimes violent game. The Frenchman, Jean Piere Javary, was red carded, reducing the home team to ten men, but when Paul Tosh collected a pass from Didier Agathe before slotting the ball past Ludovic Roy into the St Mirren goal, the home fans thought that justice had been done. Unfortunately, St Mirren had the promotion luck and a late Junior Mendes goal secured the three points for the visitors. The Paisley Buddies won 1-2.

Before the game with Inverness Caledonian Thistle, the Honorary President, John Urquhart, performed the official re-opening ceremony for the main stand. Some of the cast of Scottish Television's long-running soap opera, *Take the High Road*, were among the guests attending the opening.

You had to pay attention when the teams were announced, as Inverness had a fair sprinkling of ex-Raith players in their ranks. Les Fridge, Barry Wilson and Kevin Byers had all worn the dark blue. The visitors certainly brightened up proceedings with their orange strip but they could not match the home team for skill or fight and Raith claimed the points in a 2-0 victory. The picture shows Jay Stein showing ex-team-mate, Barry Wilson, how it is done.

Left: The club electrician, Peter Scott, brought Pratt Street to a standstill when he noticed that the north-east pylon had started to tilt. The emergency services closed Pratt Street until temporary repairs were completed, to make the leaning pylon safe. Peter had the unenviable task of dismantling the floodlights and when the pylon was made safe and repaired, he had to haul each fitting back up to the gantry, re-position and gun each lamp, then rewire them all. He is a very brave skilled electrician.

Below: The club employed the skills of the Thai practioner, Ken Anderson, who has worked on many top sports stars. Ken blames 95% of sports injuries on over tight muscles (if your muscles are over tight, the lymphatic system does not flow around the body, which affects your brain as well as your body). Ken's technique looks a bit weird and painful but his 'patient', Kenny Black, told me that any discomfort was worth it for the results the therapy produced.

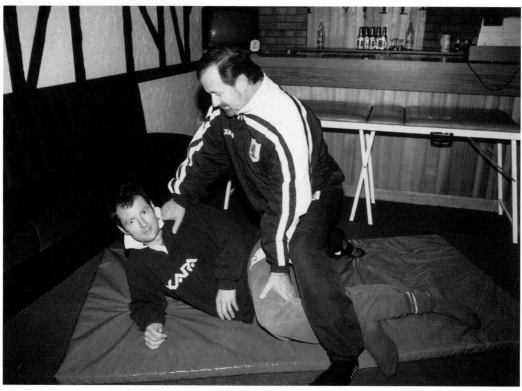

Above: Raith beat the transfer deadline to secure the services of the Canadian international Paul Fenwick, who signed a short-term contract to see the end of the season out with the Rovers. Admitting to having had a fall out with Morton, Paul was happy to be able to train regularly with Raith and, hopefully, put himself in the shop window. The classy defender went on to join Hibernian the following season.

Right: Ansah Owusu joined Raith on a short-term loan from Wimbledon and, in the seven games he played for Raith, the north London lad managed to score three goals, including one against Livingston. Unfortunately the rest of the forward line were firing blanks and the Rovers started to drop down the league.

Visitors Clydebank wrapped up the league fixtures for season 1999/00. The visitors had managed only one win all season and, embarrassingly enough, that team just happened to be Raith Rovers. The season had been another disaster for the home side: losing a manager under weird circumstances, missing out on promotion to the top division, with St Mirren promoted as Champions alongside second placed ('whisper it, Dunfermline'). But look on the bright side, we had not been relegated, we finished higher in the league than last season and at least the 'Pars' could not beat us. The season had been a successful failure but at least Peter Hetherston had been able to cut his managerial teeth, the new board had made inroads into sorting out the club's finances and Raith were still there to fight another day. Relegated Clydebank managed a 0-0 draw and the picture shows the ex-Rover, Ian Cameron, trying to outwit Craig McEwan.

It was not all glum faces on the last day of the season. I managed to pry Gordon Holmes out of the pie stand to present the prizes to the winners and runners up of the half-time penalty-kick competition. Sometimes the half-time efforts of the youngsters were more entertaining than the game. The competition was organised by Ian Stewart of the supporters' club and had been sponsored for a number of seasons by Gordon Holmes' employers, the *Fife Free Press*.

five

If you're good enough, you're old enough

The full squad at the start of season 2000/01.

The vast majority of supporters were, to say the least, relieved that although we had not won promotion, Raith Rovers were still in business. To help keep the club afloat, Archie Smith, the owner and managing director of the club's main sponsor, Fife Fabrication, was invited to join the board. This photograph was taken on the day of the announcement and shows, from left to right: Colin McGowan (finance director), Eric Drysdale (company secretary), Willie Gray (chairman), Christie Smith (Archie's wife), Ruby Anne Gray (Willie's wife) and Archie Smith.

The new club captain, Alex Burns, said in the match programme that the team had to take points off the so-called lowly teams (like Alloa). Unfortunately no one told Alloa, and the visitors won 1-2.

That game against Alloa was a warning of things to come. Marvin Andrews had returned late from the summer break, after his agent had punted him around as many clubs as he could. The manager, Peter Hetherston, eventually found out that he had been training with Sheffield Wednesday. Jean-Phillipe Javary had a spell at Birmingham – Peter knew about that, but the Andrew's situation had made his planning and team selection difficult and that had spilled over onto the pitch. Andy Clark tried hard to get his name on the score sheet, but it was his replacement, Ivan Mballa, who scored Raith's only goal. Even the late returning Marvin Andrews was brought on for Javary, and played up front in an effort to salvage a point.

Left: The Pratt family were well-represented at 'Pratt Street' on the day of the Alloa game. Our mascots for the day lining up with Roary Rover are, from left to right: five-year-old Isobel Pratt, seven-year-old James Pratt and three-year-old Sheila Pratt.

Below: Sacha Opinel wins this dual with ex-Rover Paul Brownlie in the second round of the CIS Cup.

The cup game with Arbroath was heading for extra time when the substitute, Gerry Creaney, was brought down as he surged into the penalty box. Alex Burns made no mistake from the spot kick to earn Raith a third round tie away to Celtic.

That win against Arbroath, which came into the workman-like category, seemed to kick-start Raith's season. Inverness were next to play Rovers in the league. The programme editor described the match as 'Raith having swept aside the challenge of Inverness Caledonian Thistle' (quite a mouthful, but that is what happens when clubs amalgamate) and that was just about spot on. Apart from a spell in the second half when I.C.T. scored their goal, it was all Raith. Despite the attentions of Bobby Mann, Paul Tosh managed to grab a goal as Rovers cruised home 4-1.

Left: Ross County fell to the same scoreline as their highland neighbours, but the buzz around the ground was for the return of Shaun Dennis, on loan from Hibs. Shaun was looking for a regular game, and manager Peter Hetherston was looking for someone to link with Marvin Andrews and Paul Browne in the defence. The fans were just happy to see 'Veg' back in the dark blue strip.

Below: The second 4-1 win saw Raith start to rise up the table, but one aspect of the team's play was obvious to all. The Frenchman, Sacha Opinel, was a very talented player, but to put it in Peter Hetherston's words, 'he's a hot head' Giving one hundred per cent is great, but not if it starts to penalise the team with unnecessary bookings and sendings off. The picture shows Sacha holding off a Ross County player, with Jay Stein in attendance.

Above: The goalkeeper, Guido van De Kamp, was almost a spectator in the last two home games, coping well with anything the opposition could throw at him. It was just as well – if Guido did make a mistake, Steve Tosh was always on hand to tell him the errors in his performance.

Right: After the two 4-1 back-to-back wins, Raith, with a sizeable travelling support, made their way to Parkhead for the third round of the CIS Cup but any good that had come from the previous games was easily wiped away as Celtic brought the Raith players back down to earth with a 0-4 win. At least the travelling fans showed their sense of humour by chanting 'we're only here for the money, here for the money!' Playing in that game was Ray McKinnon – the ex-Dundee United player was hoping for a contract with Raith. In the next game at Falkirk, Ray was red carded for a handling offence in the box.

That cup defeat knocked some of the stuffing out of Raith and they lost that next game at Brockville 1-2. The league fixtures had Raith on the road to Livingston the following week and I must admit I did not for one minute think that we would beat the league leaders. In fact, I would happily have accepted a share of the points before kick-off, but Raith had other ideas and they turned in a champagne performance to win 4-0. Big Marvin Andrews had scored Raith's only goal against Falkirk the week before, but he went one better against Livingston, with a brace. Paul Tosh and Alex Burns scored the other goals.

Pictured with the team captains and referee W.S.G. Young, is the match mascot, Gary Baynham, and the special guests for the game with Morton, the Lang Toun Lad and Lass. Unfortunately they did not bring the team any luck and Morton won 0-1. Significantly, this was to be the last game for the captain, Alex Burns, as he and fellow team-mates Marvin Andrews and Steve Tosh were all transferred to Livingston. The trio, probably Raith's best players, were transferred to the league leaders to reduce the crippling wage bill and to bring in, albeit a small amount, of cash to the struggling club. Had the trio gone to a team in a higher division, or even to an English side, the fans would not have been quite so upset, but to go to promotion rivals was just too much for some fans to swallow.

With the heart ripped out of the team it was a surprise to no one when the results started to go against them. A hard fought 0-0 draw at Broadwood was followed by a 1-3 defeat at home to Ayr United. Gerard Thomas Creaney, Gerry to his mates, had signed a three-month contract at the start of the season and, it was hoped that Gerry's skill and experience would help settle the side. If Gerry's time at Kirkcaldy is remembered for anything it would be the penalty that he 'won' against Arbroath in the CIS Cup, which took Raith to his old stomping ground of Parkhead.

Revenge, some say, is sweet. Raith got their revenge against Alloa for beating them in the opening league fixture of the season, when they took the trip through to Recreation Park, although it was more a case of revenge is sweat, as Raith slogged out a 1-0 win. At least Rovers were back to winning ways and the manager Peter Hetherston hoped the team would finally get into the winning habit. Airdrie put that hope on hold as the Diamonds earned a 1-1 draw. Andy Clark, starting his third game in a row, worked hard but could not get his name on the score sheet, although the Celtic target, Paul Shields, did.

Above: If you ever wanted to see a photograph that emphasised youth and experience, this is it. The veteran, Kenny Black, guards the post while youngster (if you're good enough you're old enough) Laurie Ellis, fights for position, as Falkirk attack the Raith goal.

Right: Another new face on the board of directors was Turnbull Hutton. Turnbull, a lifetime Raith Rovers fan, was the man behind 'Final Blend' – the whisky produced to commemorate the Coca-Cola Cup final against Celtic.

Right: Despite losing 0–2 to Falkirk, the central defender Paul Browne (centre of picture), was voted Man of the Match by the match sponsor, Harry Cairns. On the left of the picture is an old workmate of mine, Tom Morgan.

Below: Renault Cars dealership 'Glenvarigill' sponsored the ballboys and ballgirl for the rest of the season.

Above: Fundraising efforts were again being stepped up to help Raith Rovers survive, and a cup winning night was organised in the Raith Suite. The BBC supplied the club with a full broadcast quality video and the supporters' club organised other money collecting ideas (I suggested they take bets on the outcome of the match, but that idea fell on deaf ears for some reason!). Note the brave gentleman in the middle of the photograph wearing the Celtic top. It had been hoped that Jimmy Nicholl, Jason Dair and Steve Crawford, all now with Dunfermline, would attend the function, but permission for the trio to attend was declined. Only Shaun Dennis, now on loan to Raith from Hibs, came along to enjoy the evening.

Right: There were more changes behind the scenes as Alan Dall took over as programme editor. Alan was virtually thrown in at the deep end and along with his wife, Jenni, and help from some new contributors (including Rio Grande) he very quickly put together a quality publication. One article in Alan's first programme was a report on the Raith Rovers Ladies team, who had travelled to Aberdeen and won 6-1.

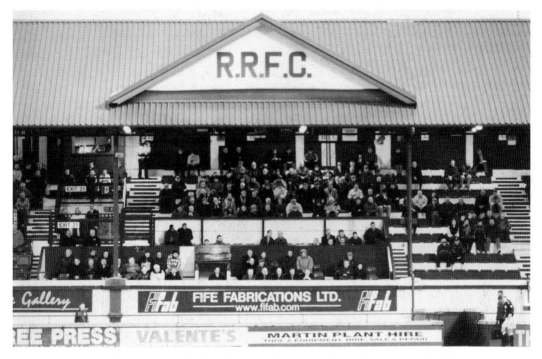

Crowds were slipping as Raith played host to Clyde on 2 December, with only 1,810 turning up. The cold weather and Christmas shopping were starting to take their toll.

Begloved Ivan Mballa gets stuck in against Alan Maitland's Clyde, who were fast becoming a bit of a jinx team for Raith, and the jinx worked again as the 'Bully Wee' won 1-2.

With funds still alarmingly short just before Christmas, the Mercat shopping centre again came to the rescue and offered the use of an empty unit in the shopping mall. As well as the usual strips, mugs and scarves on sale, I organised a 'guess the mascot's birthday' competition, with a top-of-the-range mountain bike as the prize. The bike, which had been donated by a local wholesaler, was won by a Mrs Barton from Burntisland. Thanks to the efforts of the supporters' club the shop was a great success and gave the club coffers a welcome boost.

In the new year all thoughts of winning promotion were slipping away fast, but to be fair, very few fans would even have considered the spectre of relegation looming large on the horizon. Raith were sitting in the middle of the table having performed slightly better away from Starks Park than at home. Morton were the bottom club with only four wins and four draws out of nineteen starts. Most people would have bet their new Christmas shirt and tie gift set on the home side grabbing both points but a stodgy 'Ton' managed to scrape a 0-0 draw.

Relegation was now staring Raith in the face as they embarked on a disastrous run of seven defeats in a row, including a 0-2 defeat at the hands of Stirling in the third round of the Scottish Cup at Forthbank. Peter Hetherston told the assembled press after the cup game that he was considering his position with the club. The fact that the players and staff had to take a 25% wage cut could not have helped the morale of anyone connected with the club. In an attempt to bolster the Raith defence the ex-Aberdeen defender, John Inglis, was drafted in. His efforts came to nothing in the game against Ross County as the highlanders won 0-4.

With Guido Van de Kamp having left the club, the reserve goalkeeper, Craig Coyle, was drafted in but he, sadly, was not the answer. The search was on for a replacement for Guido. More players were signed on short-term contracts in an attempt to stave off relegation. One of those signings was Paddy Kelly. Paddy had been a 'future prospect' with Celtic but, with the Glasgow club having so many changes of managers, he had tried his luck in England with Newcastle, and was then on loan to Reading, before finding his way back to his home town club (he was brought up just a few doors away from where I live) via Livingston.

Raith Rovers Independent Supporters Trust was set up to help secure the future of the club and they chipped in with a cheque for £2,500. The chairman, Willie Gray, accepted the donation on behalf of the club.

This is the team that took the field against Inverness C.T. which included two Frenchmen, goalkeeper Sammy Monin, and midfielder Wilfred Nanou. Both players soon became favourites of the dwindling home support and wee Willie showed some entertaining skill to the beleaguered fans.

Above: Raith had managed to stop the rot and had now embarked on a run of three drawn games, 0-0 at home to Falkirk, 1-1 away to Morton and 1-1 at home to Inverness. The real shock though, was when the League leaders, Livingston, paid us a visit. Sammy Monin stopped everything Livingston could throw at him and two goals from Mark Jones gave Raith three much needed points and restored some pride.

Right: The Spaniards, Salvador Capin and Miquel Alfonso, had been signed from crisis club Airdrie (there was more than one). Even the class of Capin could not help Raith beat bogey club Clyde the 'Bully Wee' as they scored the only goal of the game. The result meant First Division survival for Clyde, but Raith were teetering on the brink of disaster.

Raith Rovers fans outnumbered the home support as Peter Hetherston took his team to Alloa. Andy Smith signed from Kilmarnock earlier in the season, opening the scoring for Rait, and Paul Tosh netted the second and decisive goal after he had missed a penalty. The Wasps did pull one back but two sendings off for the home side made their task impossible.

The last home game of the season brought Airdrie to Kirkcaldy and, in a cup style game, Jay Stein put the question of relegation out of the heads of everyone who was connected with the home side, with a magnificent hat-trick in the 5-0 win. As far as the Rovers fans were concerned that was that: we were safe, the last game of the season away to Ross County did not matter (thank goodness, as the Dingwall side took four goals from Raith with no reply). This was the second time in three seasons that we had just managed to scrape out of the relegation zone and I prayed to God that I would not have to go through that again. It was a prayer that I am sure every Rovers fan, player and official was murmuring under his or her breath.

six

From relegation
to celebration

The first team squad for season 2001/02. From left to right, back row: G. Robertson (coach), Jorge Zoco, John Rushford, Andy Clark, Sammy Monin, Simon Miotto, Paul Browne, Andy Smith, Laurie Ellis, Paul Greene (physio). Front row: Nacho Novo, Ross Matheson, George O'Boyle, Wilfred Nanou, Peter Hetherston (manager), Danny Smith (chairman), Kenny Black (assistant manager), Shaun Dennis, Jay Stein, Greg McCulloch, Paul Hampshire.

Newly promoted Partick Thistle were Raith's first visitors for the first home league game of a season that just had to be better than the one before. The following Tuesday, Partick returned on Bell's Cup duty, after having inflicted a 1-2 defeat on the home side. Although Raith started off well, the game ended 3-5 in favour of the visitors after extra time, with the new Spanish signings, Nacho Novo (seen here getting stuck in with Gerry Britton) and Jorge Zoco both getting their names on the score sheet.

Above: The 'Aussie' goalkeeping coach, Simon Miotto, had taken over in goal from Sammy Monin and helped steady the Raith defence. Two away trips to Dingwall (0-1) and Ayr (1-1), were followed up by a visit to Starks Park by Falkirk.

Right: The ex-Hearts star, Scott Crabbe, had joined the club on loan from Livingston and he was turning in some excellent displays.

Shaun Dennis celebrates as Scott Crabbe scores one of his two goals of the Rovers' 5-2 result against Falkirk. Nacho Novo (2) and Jay Stein were the home side's other scorers.

It was not just Raith Rovers fixtures that the club's supporters travelled to. Raith can boast a large contingent of loyal Tartan Army fans and I am proud to say that my son, Greig, is a serving member.

Right: Arbroath were propping up the table (with Raith just two points above them) with five league games played, and Rovers did themselves a power of good, earning a 3-1 home win. Here, Scott Crabbe is whipping a cross into the box with the ex-Raith player, Paul Brownlie, doing a puppet-on-a-string impersonation.

Below: 'Our best performance this season', was the quote from the manager Peter Hetherston, as his team put three past St Mirren with no reply from the visitors.

Back in September, Raith had produced a sluggish display in the CIS Cup against Montrose, winning 1-0. They had managed to dispose of Falkirk 2-0 at Brockville in round two, earning themselves a home draw against Hibs. Raith were not at their best after two disappointing league results, going down 2-3 at Clyde and scrapping a 2-2 draw at home to league leaders Airdrie, and things were not getting any better when ex-Rover, Craig Brewster, put two goals past Sammy Monin, despite Laurie Ellis's efforts.

Raith had fallen to second bottom after two successive away defeats: 1-2 against Partick Thistle and 0-1 at Falkirk. So a point at home against Ayr at least stopped the losing streak. This photograph looks like it shows Nacho Novo scoring against Craig Nelson, but it was a header from Shaun Dennis (out of shot) that secured that valuable point.

In front of only 1,468 fans, Raith were crushed 1-5 at home to Inverness C.T., the only highlight being Nacho Novo's penalty after he was brought down in the box. 'Only one team wanted to win that game and they were not in dark blue jerseys' was Peter Hetherston's comment after the game!

'This lot do it quite simply for the love of the club', was the caption appearing with the photograph of the supporters' club committee, when it was printed in the matchday programme. From left to right, back row: Jim McIntosh, Bill Brown, Eddie Doig, Ian Stewart, John Taylor, Kenny Grainlee. Front row: Linda Bell, Fraser Hamilton, Jim Foy (chairman), Gordon Adamson, Ken Jeffrey, Liz Alison.

Left: With Raith deep in relegation trouble, the club tried to generate much needed funds by opening a shop for the Christmas period in the Mercat Centre, and most of our foreign players turned up for the opening. Pictured with two young fans are: Paquito, Nanou, Javary, Monin, Tajero, Novo and Zoco.

Below: With most fans crying into their Christmas pudding at the club's predicament, these youngsters from the Junior Rovers section managed to have a great time at the Christmas party.

In 2002, Jocky Scott was brought in to replace Peter Hetherston as manager, in an attempt to lift Raith off the bottom slot in Division One.

By mid-March there had been no turnaround in the Kirkcaldy club's fortunes. Partick Thistle sat proudly at the top of Division One and Raith sat at the bottom. Nacho Novo and Andy Smith tried hard, but even their efforts were in vain.

Above: Rovers had to win their last game against Ross County to have a chance of staying up, as second top Airdrie were about to fold. Had they won and Falkirk lost their match, Raith's superior goal difference could have saved the club from relegation. However, despite the home side's best efforts, it did not work out. Raith were relegated, Airdrie went out of business and Falkirk stayed up by default.

Left: The Raith Rovers board had to look to the future and, for season 2002/03, they chose the Spanish duo, Antonio Calderon and Francisco Ortiz (Paquito), to take Raith back to Divison One.

Opposite below: The pre-season signings, Martin Prest and Raul Ojeda, posed with Paul Browne and Ian Brown for this publicity photograph for the club's main sponsors, 'Bar Itza'. Two Scots, an Argentinian and a Spaniard dressed as Mexicans? I am glad our main sponsors were not 'Andrex' or 'Toilet Duck'!

Above: The 2002/03 squad. From left to right, back row: W. Nanou, S. Paliczka, R. Matheson, C. Boylin, A. Moffat, I. Brown, B. Carrigan, S. Miller, L. Ellis, P. Green (physiotherapist). Middle row: J. Mas, P. Hampshire, P. Parkin, J. Sweeney, R. Ojeda, S. Monin, A. Davidson, A. Smith, D. Brady. Front row: K. Hawley, D. Ross, S. Dennis, A. Calderon (player/manager), D. Smith (chairman), Paquito (player/assistant manager), P. Browne, M. Prest, R. Blackadder.

Left: Another pre-season signing (but not for the team) was the lifelong Raith fan, Gavin Quinn. Resplendent in full Raith Rovers tartan, one of 'Fife's Finest', Gavin signed for life, along with his fiancée, Lorraine.

Below: The new 'goalie', Raul Ojeda, is in pre-season action against Dundee.

Above: After a shaky start (Raith had drawn the first two league fixtures 1-1 at home to Stranraer and away to Berwick, with a 0-3 defeat at the hands of Airdie United in the Bell's Challenge Cup), Antonio's charges finally picked up three points in the 1-0 victory over Dumbarton. Ian Brown put in a solid performance in defence.

Right: During the season, pre-match entertainment was often provided by Jack Smith, the son of the Raith striker, Andy. Jack's ball-juggling skills were a joy to watch (perhaps he is one to watch for the future).

After a humiliating 1-3 defeat away to Cowdenbeath the home side took on the ex-manager, John McVeigh's, Stenhousemuir. Antonio Calderon, having recovered from a long-term injury problem, helped guide Raith to victory. Andy Smith scored the only goal of the game.

The CIS League Cup draw gave Rovers a home tie against First Division Alloa, but despite pulling back a two goal deficit, with goals from Prest and Carrigan (pictured celebrating), Raith lost the tie 2-3.

After going bust Airdrie reformed as Airdrie United, thanks to the takeover of Clydebank. Rovers piled on the pressure but United's defence held out for a 0-0 draw. Karl Hawley came close to breaking the deadlock from this free-kick.

The club mascot, Roary Rover, shows off the new away strip. The chairman Danny Smith and finance director Colin McGowan point to where all Mario Caira's pies went.

Left: By the time Berwick Rangers visited Kirkcaldy, Raith had produced an unbeaten run of home league games. Despite the efforts of Brian Carrigan, the team from England put paid to that, producing a workman-like 1-2 defeat on the home side, helping to knock Raith off the top spot in the table.

Below: Named as the Bell's player of the month for October, Ryan Blackadder was attracting the attention of a number of clubs. 'Dude's' goal against Cowdenbeath was described as a 'wonder volley'. The 4-1 win helped to wipe out the memory of the Fife rivals first encounter of the season.

Before the game with Hamilton Accies, PA announcer Gordon Adamson interviews the match mascots Bryan Grieve and George Wilson.

Hard on the heels of an uncomfortable 1-1 draw with Hamilton came Raith's biggest win of the season so far: the result was 5-1 against Forfar. Signed from East Fife, Paul McManus managed a brace of goals in his first full start for the club.

Also back in goal for Raith was the previous season's regular goalkeeper, Sammy Monin, who is seen here getting some help from his defence and also Andy Smith. Sammy was unhappy at not being first choice goalkeeper and when he was dropped to the bench for the league game at Brechin he walked out of the stadium; his contract was cancelled by mutual agreement the following Monday.

In the new year in the second half of the league campaign, Raith were sitting at the top of the table, seven points clear of Berwick. Rovers finally managed to score against Airdrie United, with Andy Smith scoring the only goal of the game.

The assistant manager, Paquito, played consistently well and won a lot of admiration for his skills and work rate. However, he did not enjoy our cold weather and often sported a pair of gloves.

It is rumoured that some fans like (or perhaps need) a small refreshment before they watch Raith play. Joe McCluskey was always happy to oblige at what is generally agreed to be 'the' Rovers pub, the Novar Bar. The bar has an amazing collection of football and Raith Rovers memorabilia on display.

When Brechin City came to Kirkcaldy, Raith were well on top of the league. City were in seventh place, but Dick Campbell had managed to sign the ex-legend, Scott Thomson, on loan from Dunfermline. Although Ray McKinnon sent an unstoppable volley past the goalkeeper, Scott then proceeded to pull off a number of great saves and goals from Grant and Templeman won all three points for the Angus side.

Shaun Dennis opened the scoring against Dumbarton as Raith started a run of three home games on the trot. Martin Prest took only another three minutes to net the second goal and Raith won 2-1.

Usually it is businesses or corporations that sponsor matches, but for the derby game against Cowdenbeath it was the alternative supporters' group 'Fife's Finest' who did the honours.

The game against the 'Blue Brazil' was always going to be a scrappy affair, with Raith looking to wrap up the title and Cowdenbeath being desperate for points to avoid relegation. The former Monaco defender, Cristian Patino, opened the scoring and stopped a number of attacks before the home side finished 2-1 ahead.

A shock 2-4 defeat away at Forfar was followed by a trip to Stenhousemuir. The visitors went behind in the first minute, but then rallied and ran out winners 3-1. This away win under their belts gave Raith confidence for the visit of Hamilton. Although Prest came close to scoring early on, it was left to Patino to score Raith's only goal in a disappointing 1-1 draw, with Shaun Dennis scoring an own goal.

Raith Rovers can also boast a successful ladies team. From left to right, back row: John Wyles (coach), P. Geatons, L. Halliday, D. Wyles, L. MacKenzie, A. Keir, S. Cuthbert, K. Scott, Y. Tindal, L. Wheatley, Eddie Doig (manager). Front row: L. Patrick, K. Thomson, C. Halliday, M. Wyles, N. Shepherd, M. Kirby, S. Lennie, N. Glover.

By the time Berwick arrived, an incredible run of two points from a possible eighteen had the fans' nerves shattered. Raith could win promotion if they claimed the three points on offer. The gaffer changed the shape of the team, pushing three up front, working tirelessly to win the match.

In the eighty-second minute, all of Raith's efforts were rewarded when Andy Smith instinctively headed the winner from a Martin Prest cross. The board members in the director's box could not contain their delight.

That last eight minutes (plus injury time) seemed to go on forever, but at the final whistle the feeling amongst the home support was as much relief as joy.

At last the captain, Shaun Dennis, proudly showed the Second Division League trophy to the fans. Then the champagne flowed!

Above: As the players and management team crowded around the board declaring Raith as Champions, the look on Antonio Calderon's face said it all. In only one season, which was his first as a manager, the team were back in Division One. It had been a nervy campaign, with some good and bad games, but the chairman's gamble of staying full-time had paid off.

Right: In my twelfth year as club photographer, I saw the club go from relegation to celebration. What would year thirteen bring? The team's T-shirts proclaimed 'El ejã´rcito azul y blanco de Calderon', (Calderon's blue and white army). Raith Rovers were back, finances were not great, but they were not as bad as some other club's. Season 2003/04 could not come quick enough for me!

Other local titles published by Tempus

Raith Rovers 1991/92-1995/96
TONY FIMISTER

Covering the most successful period in the club's history, this photographic record is an essential item for anyone with an interest in Raith Rovers. It contains over 200 illustrations, many of which have never previously been published, and detailed captions documenting the golden era at Starks Park.
7524 2425 4

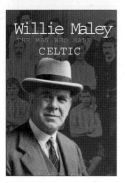

Willie Maley The Man Who Made Celtic
DAVID W. POTTER

Having starred in the early Celtic teams of the 1880s, Willie Maley went on to be an inspirational figure in the development of the club. Eventually becoming the manager at Parkhead, he moulded Celtic into one of the finest club sides in the world and continued to lead them until the 1930s, presiding over many epic victories and a wealth of trophies.
7524 2691 5

Edinburgh Under Siege 1571-1573
HARRY POTTER

In 1571 Edinburgh was at the centre of a bloody siege in which many men sacrificed their lives in support of the dethroned Queen Mary. William Kirkcaldy and Wililiam Maitland held the castle against a succession of regents. In despair the Earl of Morton turned to the English to overthrow the Castle rebels. Within ten days the English cannons and a thousand men brought the rebels to their knees and the majestic towers of the citadel crumbled around them.
7524 2332 0

Flodden
NIALL BARR

This infamous battle was the scene where Scotland's 'rose nobill' – James IV – lost his life to Henry VIII's army as he courageously, and perhaps recklessly, led his own into the battlefield. While Niall Barr looks at the revolutionary nature of the battle in terms of the way it was fought, he also examines the political and social forces that caused these two old enemies to clash once more.
7524 2593 5

If you are interested in purchasing other books published by Tempus, or in case you have difficulty finding any Tempus books in your local bookshop, you can also place orders directly through our website

www.tempus-publishing.com

or from BOOKPOST, Freepost, PO Box 29, Douglas, Isle of Man, IM99 1BQ
tel 01624 836000 email bookshop@enterprise.net